IT'S JUST
MERCURY
IN
RETROGRADE

IT'S JUST MERCURY IN RETROGRADE

A JOURNAL FOR BANISHING CELESTIAL CHAOS AND PICKING UP GOOD VIBES

CHRONICLE BOOKS
680 SECOND STREET
SAN FRANCISCO, CA 94107

ISBN 978-1-7972-0071-2

Manufactured in China.

Text by Dena Rayess.
Art by Stacie Bloomfield.
Design by Rachel Harrell.
Typeset in Filson Soft.

10 9 8 7 6 5 4 3 2 1

Chronicle books and gifts are available at special quantity
discounts to corporations, professional associations, literacy
programs, and other organizations. For details and discount
information, please contact our premiums department at
corporatesales@chroniclebooks.com or at 1-800-759-0190.

Chronicle Books LLC
680 Second Street
San Francisco, California 94107
www.chroniclebooks.com

Replied all
to an email?

Said the
wrong thing?

Simply feeling
out of sorts?

It's not you, it's just Mercury in retrograde!

You may be asking yourself, *What is Mercury in retrograde anyway?*

Mercury passes around the Sun at a faster speed than Earth, so when Mercury passes Earth in orbit, from our vantage point, it looks like it's moving backward—it's essentially a cosmic optical illusion. This retrograde phenomenon lasts about 3 weeks and happens 3 to 4 times a year, which is a serious chunk of time!

OK, but why does everyone freak out about it so much?

Mercury, named after the Roman god of the same name, is the planet of communication. Think emails, phone calls, body language, or simply talking—Mercury rules it all! So when it looks like things are literally going backward in the universe, it can make us feel like everything is out of sorts.

The popular reaction to retrograde-induced mishaps is to curse the season and muddle through the day. But Mercury in retrograde can *actually* be a good thing.

Those weeks in retrograde can be an empowering time—the key is knowing what to focus on. Because communication skills can be a little shaky in the retrograde period, it's the perfect time to look inward: refocusing on your goals, taking moments for self-reflection, and renewing your spirit.

And this journal is here to help with just that. Fill out the prompts as you work through the journal or flip to one at random when the time feels right. Whether or not you're in personal retrograde, use this space to help you navigate through all your cosmic moments, big and small.

Take a walk outside today—around the block, for
5 minutes, or for 5 miles—whatever gets you breathing
the fresh air.

What did you see?

_____

_____

_____

_____

_____

_____

_____

_____

_____

_____

_____

_____

_____

_____

_____

_____

_____

_____

_____

_____

_____

What would you do if you could take yourself on a date?

_____

_____

_____

_____

_____

_____

_____

_____

_____

_____

_____

_____

_____

_____

_____

_____

_____

_____

_____

_____

_____

_____

_____

_____

Pause. Take 3 deep breaths, *then* start writing.

Make a list of your favorite guilty-pleasure songs (bonus points if you listen to them while making this list).

_____

_____

_____

_____

_____

_____

_____

_____

_____

_____

_____

_____

_____

_____

_____

_____

_____

_____

_____

_____

_____

_____

What instantly makes you feel at home?

Write out a favorite poem, quote, or song—one that makes you feel happy.

_____

_____

_____

_____

_____

_____

_____

_____

_____

_____

_____

_____

_____

_____

_____

_____

_____

_____

_____

_____

_____

_____

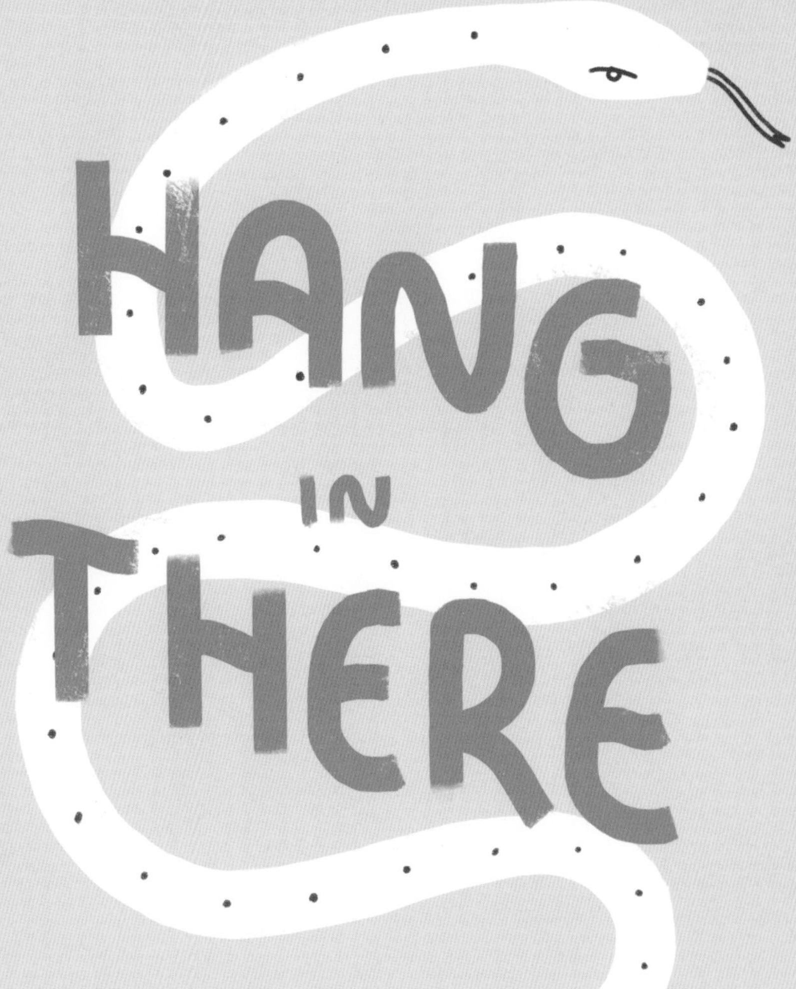
HANG
IN
THERE

It's not all bad out there. What went right in your world today?

_____

_____

_____

_____

_____

_____

_____

_____

_____

_____

_____

_____

_____

_____

_____

_____

_____

_____

_____

_____

_____

_____

_____

Make a list of your top 5 short-term goals.

THE STARS ARE WITH YOU

Plan it out: What are some of your dream vacations?

_____

_____

_____

_____

_____

_____

_____

_____

_____

_____

_____

_____

_____

_____

_____

_____

_____

_____

_____

_____

_____

_____

_____

_____

_____

_____

Self-love is the best love. Make a list of 5 (or 10, or 20!) things you love about yourself.

_____

_____

_____

_____

_____

_____

_____

_____

_____

_____

_____

_____

_____

_____

_____

_____

_____

_____

_____

_____

_____

_____

_____

_____

REST IS BEST

Is there someone you follow on social media that makes you feel crummy? Declutter your digital life and unfollow them.

_____

_____

_____

_____

_____

_____

_____

_____

_____

_____

_____

_____

_____

_____

_____

_____

_____

_____

_____

_____

_____

_____

_____

Make a list of your top 5 long-term goals. What is the first step in making each goal a reality?

_____

_____

_____

_____

_____

_____

_____

_____

_____

_____

_____

_____

_____

_____

_____

_____

_____

_____

_____

_____

_____

_____

_____

_____

Write out a recipe for your favorite comfort food. Try making it today.

_____

_____

_____

_____

_____

_____

_____

_____

_____

_____

_____

_____

_____

_____

_____

_____

_____

_____

_____

_____

_____

_____

What's something you can let go of today?

_____

_____

_____

_____

_____

_____

_____

_____

_____

_____

_____

_____

_____

_____

_____

_____

_____

_____

_____

_____

_____

_____

_____

_____

_____

Make yourself a mantra for the week—a word, phrase, or pep talk—whatever you want to come back to you when you need a boost.

_____

_____

_____

_____

_____

_____

_____

_____

_____

_____

_____

_____

_____

_____

_____

_____

_____

_____

_____

Safe space: What's something that is really bugging you today?

_____
_____
_____
_____
_____
_____
_____
_____
_____
_____
_____
_____
_____
_____
_____
_____
_____
_____
_____
_____
_____
_____
_____
_____
_____

SLOW DOWN

It's OK. Let it out.